by
Deb Mercier

Minneapolis, Minnesota

DEDICATION

For Uncle Jeff, inventor of Thumpsquish and the Agapillar and storyteller extraordinaire

ACKNOWLEDGEMENTS

Thanks to Ryan Jacobson and Lake 7 Creative, LLC, for bringing this book to life. Seeing the transformation has been amazing! Thanks also to my family and coworkers for putting up with my beastly side as the book took shape.

Edited by Dana Kuznar
Cover art by Morgan Hoff-Golmen
Cover logo by Shane Nitzsche

Photo credits: See pages 94–95.

Library of Congress Control Number: 2014947787

Copyright 2014 by Deb Mercier
Published by Lake 7 Creative, LLC
Minneapolis, MN 55412
www.lake7creative.com

All rights reserved
Printed in the USA

ISBN: 978-1-940647-13-5

Real Stories About Werewolves

PREFACE

Stories about humans transforming into wolves date back thousands of years. The wolf—one of the most feared and admired predators—plays a big role in myths and legends from around the globe, especially in the European region. In written form, the word "werewolf" or "man-wolf" was first recorded in Old English in the eleventh century.

Different cultures developed varying names for the creature. In France, the werewolf is called a *loup-garou*; in Italy a *lupo mannaro*; in Iceland a *varulfur*. However, if you saw one, you'd likely just call it *terrifying*.

In general, stories about werewolves involve either an involuntary transformation or one that is voluntary; or rather, those who are cursed or born into their affliction versus those who transform purposefully through dark and twisted methods.

This book focuses less on the specific method of transformation and more on the encounter itself: What would it feel like to actually see a werewolf in person?

And that brings us back to *terrifying*.

The stories retold here have been gathered from a variety of places. They come from encyclopedias of the strange, books of the bizarre, and the ultimate sharing space of the Internet.

While the bones of these stories remain intact, they've been embellished with the flesh and blood of everyday life. Some names have been changed and, in places, details have been added to help tell the story—to really put the reader into the characters' shoes as they encounter the inexplicable.

Enjoy!

—D.M.

A BRIEF HISTORY

Stories of werewolves date back more than 2,000 years. No one knows who invented the monster—or if those stories were based on real sightings—but quite possibly the oldest known werewolf legend comes from Greek Mythology. It was said that King Lycaon of Arcadia wished to test the god Zeus's omniscience, so he served Zeus roasted flesh from a human. As punishment for the misdeed, Zeus turned Lycaon into a wolf.

Roman mythology, too, had werewolf tales to share. Among them was a man named Moeris. According to the poet Virgil, Moeris used special herbs to change himself into a wolf.

By the 430s A.D., werewolves had moved out of mythology and into history, sort of. Some accounts claim that Saint Patrick brought lycanthropy to Ireland. When King Vereticus of Wales would not convert to Christianity, Saint Patrick cursed him, turning the king into a werewolf.

For many hundreds of years thereafter, rumors of werewolves festered throughout Europe. By the 1500s, accusations ran rampant, and countless people were tried, convicted, and usually executed for being werewolves.

Meanwhile, across the Atlantic Ocean, many Native American tribes believed in the power of shape-shifting. Perhaps best known, some Diné (Navajo People) were said to turn into wolves. These shape-shifters could also reportedly become different animals, such as birds, and could even take the forms of other humans.

The 1800s saw werewolves get the literary treatment, as entertainment. While the number of accusations and trials died down, interest in the beasts began to soar—thanks in large part to a modest little story that we now call "Little Red Riding Hood," published in 1812 by the Brothers Grimm.

Today, werewolves are ingrained in pop culture. From books and movies to sightings and encounters, werewolves—whether they be real or imagined—are never far from our collective consciousness.

TALES FROM
THE AGES

1
GIVE THAT HUNTER A HAND

France

This tale has been passed down in France, told beside countless firesides in the dead of night. While no specific year or time period is attached to the legend, it hearkens back to the days of French royalty.

Antoine entered the great hall, feeling the summer sun slip from his shoulders as he stepped into the relative gloom of the court of the Lord and Lady Roulange. Lord Roulange sat at the end of the hall on a modest throne, waiting to hear Antoine's petition.

Antoine dropped to one knee, briefly, then stood patiently, his head bowed.

"What is your reason for visiting?" asked Roulange.

Antoine raised his eyes and spoke. "If it pleases you, I ask permission to hunt game in your forests."

He caught movement behind Lord Roulange's throne. Lady Roulange emerged from the shadows behind her husband, although Antoine could swear she wasn't there a moment ago. She wore a thin circlet of gold on her head, and one of her pale, slender hands sparkled with a ring encrusted with emeralds, rubies, and the darkest of blue sapphires. She offered her hand to Antoine, who knelt again and kissed the ring to show his loyalty.

"Of course, you may hunt our lands," she said, her voice surprisingly strong. "All we ask is that you bring some of your good fortune to us at the end of your hunt."

"Thank you, Lady. Thank you, Lord," said Antoine. "I shall return in no more than a fortnight's time."

He left the great hall, glad to be back under the sun and in open air.

Over the next few days, as Antoine tracked his prey, he felt a tingling in his spine, as if somehow he were being watched. He slept little during those nights.

One morning, just before daybreak, Antoine yawned as he stepped lightly through the thick mat of forest leaves and twigs. He carried his bow with practiced ease, knowing he'd have it ready within a second if needed.

The forest to his left exploded with a sudden crash of snapping branches. Antoine barely had a chance to see the dark form leap straight for his throat.

He thrust up an arm just in time to deflect the worst of the deadly attack, stumbling under the weight of the creature as it fell to the ground and rolled back onto its paws.

Antoine saw now that it was a wolf—oddly shaped with lanky limbs and intelligent, gold-flecked eyes. Its lips curled back in a snarl.

With a hunter's instinct, Antoine knew it would attack again. In a blur of motion, he brought up his bow, just as the wolf leaped. The arrow shot fast and straight, and the wolf screeched in pain.

In an instant it was gone, disappearing back into the depths of the forest. But its paw lay on the ground, still warm and bleeding, shot off by Antoine's arrow.

After wiping the paw on the ground to remove some of the blood, Antoine placed it inside the bag he usually used for small game. He would return it to the Lord and Lady, he decided, and warn them of the savage beast inhabiting their land.

That night, Antoine sat by his campfire, the flames crackling enough to keep him company. He thought back on the strange way the wolf had behaved—it was like no other wolf he'd ever encountered. Most ran away from humans; this one attacked. Most wanted nothing to do with confrontation; this one seemed determined to fight.

He pulled his small game bag close and reached inside to remove the paw. He wanted to see it again.

His fingers touched something smooth and cold. He cried out in surprise and dropped the bag. A slender hand, white as marble, spilled out. By the light of the fire, a ring sparkled. It was encrusted with emeralds, rubies, and the darkest of blue sapphires.

The following day dawned bright but cold. Antoine shivered as he once again stood outside the great hall. He clutched his small game bag to his chest.

Once inside the gloom, he needed a moment for his eyes to adjust before he could see Lord Roulange, sitting on his throne. It was as if he hadn't moved since the last time Antoine had come. Lady Roulange stood beside her husband's throne, one hand resting lightly on the back, the other tucked demurely in a fashionable wrap.

Antoine swallowed hard, then walked quickly to the end of the room where his fate awaited.

"And how did your hunt fare?" asked Lady Roulange. Antoine could barely speak, pinned under her stare. Her eyes were flecked with gold.

"I—it was—that is . . . I was attacked by a wolf. I shot off its paw. Only—well—later, when I looked at the paw again . . ." Antoine thrust the bag at Lord Roulange. "Forgive me!" he cried.

Lord Roulange stood, taking the bag in confusion. "What do you mean by this, huntsman?" he demanded. Roulange looked into the bag, and his face paled. He drew out the hand, staring at the ring.

Lady Roulange began backing into the shadows. Her husband grabbed her arm, and she cried out in pain. The wrap fell away to reveal a bloody stump.

Her husband called for the guards.

"I'm sorry," Antoine said. He repeated it over and over as Lady Roulange was led away.

She looked back over her shoulder and smiled, her teeth long and white. "I don't blame you," she said.

The Lady was executed by nightfall.

2
CHILD'S PLAY

Germany

While no specific date is attached to this tale, it's been passed down through countless generations in the Klein Krams area of Germany, near Ludwigslust.

The great hunt, at last, thought the young cavalry officer. He'd been hinting that he wanted to take part in the hunt for years; now he'd finally been invited.

As he sat atop his horse and surveyed the land around him, he felt an overwhelming sense of pride—and more than a little excitement. This hunt was revered as a true test of prowess; sportsmen from all over Germany vied for a spot in the traditional hunt each year.

The view from atop the hill was stunning. Thick forests stretched as far as the eye could see, offering every hue of green imaginable. Behind the officer, a village bustled with life.

Another huntsman sidled up to the officer. His beard was beginning to gray, and his eyes sparkled with humor. "Your first great hunt?" asked the huntsman.

"Yes," said the officer. "You?"

The huntsman laughed. "Oh, no, I've been to several in my time." He pointed to his beard. "The proof is in the gray."

They sat quietly for a moment. Then the young officer asked with a grin, "Is it true what they say about the beast—the great wolf?"

The officer had meant it as a joke, but the huntsman leveled him with a stare. "I've seen it," he said quietly.

In recent years, dark tales had trickled from the huntsmen of Klein Krams: tales of a great wolf that interfered with the hunt. No matter how many shots were fired, no bullet seemed to find its mark on the beast, even though it came within an easy distance.

Once, the beast had even made a mockery of the huntsmen, dashing in to snatch a hunk of meat off their kill and sliding back into the forest, unharmed.

The officer couldn't tell if the huntsman was joking or not. He shifted on his horse. "You're saying you saw this beast yourself?" he asked.

"I took aim and fired," said the huntsman. "It was in my sights, and there was no way I could've missed. In fact . . ." He paused.

"Go on," said the officer.

"I swear; it . . . grinned at me," said the huntsman. "But that was another time," he added abruptly. "Good luck." He coaxed his horse into a run and left the officer with his own uneasy thoughts.

The next day dawned bright and clear, a crisp and perfect morning to launch the great hunt. The young cavalry officer rode his horse through the village to the meeting point, his horse's hooves drumming up puffs of dust. Houses lined either side of the road.

Suddenly, a group of children streamed from a house to the right, running and screaming as if the Devil himself were after them. The officer's horse remained steady, and the officer could see nothing nearby to cause them such fright.

Curious, he caught up to the last child and stopped him. "What frightened you?"

The boy gasped for breath, glancing over his shoulder at a house down the road. "It's the Feeg family, sir. They left him at home by himself again."

"What do you mean?" asked the officer.

"The youngest—he shouldn't be alone."

"Why not?"

"When he's left alone, he turns into a wolf. He does it every time, and every time we run. No one wants to get bit."

The officer smiled and nodded knowingly. "I see. Run and catch your friends."

The boy took off like a shot, and the officer grinned again. *Nothing like a game of "Big Bad Wolf and the Sheep" when you're a child,* he thought. He urged his horse back down the road.

The door on the house from which the children had run stood open, swinging slightly in the breeze.

That's odd, thought the officer.

He slowed as he approached and peered into the house's interior. His stomach gave a jolt. Staring at him from the doorway was a large black wolf.

As he passed the house, he shook his head. He looked back. Now, staring at him from the doorway was a small, pale boy with dark, shaggy hair.

"Werwolf" by Lucas Cranach the Elder

3

REAL WEREWOLVES OR FORCED CONFESSIONS?

As the two previous stories suggest, history is ripe with a surprising number of reported sightings and strange encounters with werewolves. To take the idea of lycanthropy a step further, there are actually a number of cases in which people confessed to being part wolf.

It can be difficult to take the confessors at their word, though. Like so many witches through the ages, most werewolves usually only confessed after being tortured—while a number of other confessions can be blamed on depraved attention-seeking or mental illness.

The following alleged accounts are some of history's most infamous werewolf stories. Were the confessions forced, or is there some truth to the claims?

WEREWOLVES OF POLIGNY—FRANCE, 1521

A man was traveling through the town of Poligny when he was attacked by a wolf. He bravely fought off the animal and was even able to wound it. The wolf escaped, and its trail of blood led directly to the home of Michel Verdung.

Verdung was questioned, and he confessed to being a werewolf. He also named Pierre Bourgot and Philibert Montot as werewolves. The trio was executed.

*****

WEREWOLF OF PAVIA—ITALY, 1541

A serial killer struck Pavia in 1541. His crimes were bloody, brutal, and savage. When the murderer was apprehended, he readily confessed to being a werewolf. But, in a bizarre twist, he explained that his wolf hair grew inside his body, beneath his skin; it wasn't visible.

The killer was sentenced to death, and his boast was tested: His body was mutilated in search of fur.

*****

WEREWOLF OF DOLE—FRANCE, 1572

After several children were kidnapped and murdered near the town of Dole, rumors began swirling of a werewolf on the prowl. Authorities issued a proclamation that allowed its citizens to hunt and kill the werewolf.

One night, a group of men came upon a terrible scene. Some accounts claim that they saw a werewolf, while others suggest they only heard it. What's certain is that they discovered another dead child.

A hermit named Gilles Garnier was arrested, and he confessed to being a werewolf. He claimed that a forest spirit appeared to him and gave him an ointment, which provided him with the ability to become a wolf.

*****

WEREWOLF OF BEDBURG—GERMANY, 1589

Peter Stubbe was a well-liked farmer in the town of Bedburg. He, and so many other farmers, seemed completely bemused by the mutilated cows that continued to turn up in the area. Unfortunately, that was nothing compared to what came next.

Things took a turn for the worse when children and young women began disappearing. Some of their bodies were later found; others never were. Most agreed that the deaths were caused by wolf attacks.

They were at least partially right. A team of hunters caught the trail of the murderous beast and tracked it for several days. When they finally cornered it, they were shocked to find that it was Peter Stubbe.

The farmer confessed to being a werewolf. Furthermore, he explained that the Devil had given him a magic belt of wolf fur. By wearing it, he became a monster.

*****

WEREWOLF OF CHALONS—FRANCE, 1598

Also nicknamed the Demon Tailor, the Werewolf of Chalons worked as a tailor by day. By night, he preyed upon children and supposedly ate them. He kept their bones in barrels hidden in his cellar.

The bones were discovered, and the tailor's dark secret was revealed. He was convicted and sentenced to death.

4
TEEN WOLF

France, 1603

One of history's most notorious werewolf trials involved a teenaged boy. Although his father lived nearby, 13-year-old Jean Grenier had been on his own for some time, earning his keep wherever he could as a servant. He was a strange boy, a loner, but no one paid him much mind.

In the southwest region of France, where Jean lived, children of the small hamlets and villages began to disappear—snatched from roads or fields and never seen again.

In one reported case, a mother left her cottage, her infant safely sleeping in a cradle. When she returned just a short time later, the baby was gone. People began to suspect that a wolf—or something much worse—was to blame.

*****

THE ATTACKS INTENSIFY

A young boy played by the edge of the forest, humming and searching for interesting sticks and rocks.

A low growl came from the woods. The boy barely had time to look up before a wolf leaped from the trees and knocked him down. The child hit the ground hard, all of his breath driven out of him. He gasped for air and tried to yell. He flailed at the wolf and felt a jarring snap as its jaws closed just inches from his throat.

The boy found his voice and screamed. Luckily, his uncle was nearby; he came running. Brandishing a heavy stick, the boy's uncle beat the wolf, landing blows until it relinquished the child and turned to its new prey with an angry snarl.

The boy's uncle would not fall easily, so the wolf soon ran back into the depths of the forest.

*****

Marguerite Poirier hated working with Jean Grenier. He was dirty and skinny, he dressed in rags, and he smelled horrendous. His nails were long and ragged like claws, especially his left thumbnail. To top it all off, Jean scared her. He kept telling her strange and gruesome tales of what he did, even bragging about the children he ate, when he went prowling as a werewolf.

One day, before she left to tend sheep with Jean, she told her parents about the stories and her fear of him. It hadn't gone well. Her father told her to quit being silly.

"That's all they are, child: stories," her mother said. "Now get you to work like a good girl."

And so Marguerite left to tend sheep, dreading her time with Jean. She tightly gripped her iron-pointed staff, her mouth set in a grim line.

When she reached the flock, Jean was nowhere to be found. She breathed a sigh of relief, chose a good vantage point, and settled in to keep watch.

Some time later, the sheep at the far edge of the flock became agitated. Marguerite shaded the sun from her eyes to better see what was disturbing them. The flock seemed to split in two, and running full speed down the middle of them—toward her—was a red-brown wolf with a short stump for a tail.

In seconds, it reached her. It circled Marguerite in a frenzy, all claws and teeth and hair-raising snarls. The girl spun with it, her iron-tipped staff always between herself and the wolf.

It lunged, and she cried out as its teeth tore through her skirt. Instinctively, she lashed out and landed a heavy blow on the wolf's back. It yelped and backed off, but still it circled, looking for a way past Marguerite's sharp staff.

She screamed and landed another blow, and another. The wolf finally broke off its attack and streaked away. It looked back as if laughing at her. Keeping her staff ready, Marguerite ran as fast as she could back home.

*****

THE TRIAL BEGINS

It was Jean Grenier himself who began piling up the evidence of his guilt in the long and gruesome string of attacks. He bragged to anyone who would listen that it was he who had terrorized Marguerite Poirier—and if not for her staff, he would have eaten her . . . just like he'd eaten the others.

After Marguerite testified, Jean was arrested and brought before the parliament of Bordeaux.

At his trial, Jean claimed to be a werewolf. He freely, proudly confessed to murdering and eating children, including the infant taken from the cradle in his home.

What came next from Jean was the strange and twisted tale of how he became a werewolf. It all started with a trip into the forest with another youth from the area, Pierre di la Tilhaire (also called Duthillaire).

Jean followed Pierre, the undergrowth snagging his feet. The moon shone brightly overhead, but the thick canopy of the trees blocked most of the light, creating silvery shadows everywhere.

Pierre stopped and held up his hand, signaling Jean to stop. "He's close," whispered Pierre.

Jean shivered with anticipation. Pierre had promised to bring him to see the Lord of the Forest.

Although neither boy heard a sound, a tall man dressed in black and riding a horse the color midnight appeared before them.

He saluted the boys and dismounted with barely a whisper. Jean stood still, as the man came closer and studied him. The man leaned down and kissed Jean on the cheek with lips as cold as ice. Then the stranger presented each of them with wolf-skins and salves that, when worn, would transform the boys into wolves.

Jean took his wolf-skin with reverence, stroking the red-brown pelt.

The dark man spoke, his voice an echoing nightmare. He told the boys to never pare the fingernails of their left thumbs, or the wolf-skin wouldn't work.

*****

EVIDENCE MOUNTS

At trial, Jean recounted specific details about the children he'd eaten: times, dates, locations, and more. The victims' families and the rare survivors of attacks stepped forward; they gave matching details.

While confessing to the court, Jean also accused his father, Pierre Grenier, of sorcery and werewolfism. The court ordered Pierre Grenier to appear, but after days of interrogation, the judge released him. Pierre Grenier, a simple man, knew nothing about his son's crimes.

*****

THE FATE OF JEAN GRENIER

Discounting the testimony of Marguerite Poirier, who said she'd been attacked by Grenier in wolf form, and dismissing Jean's claims of becoming a werewolf, the judge called in two doctors to examine Jean.

The doctors both pronounced to the court that Jean suffered from lycanthropy—but that he only thought he was a werewolf.

Taking Jean's youth into consideration, the judge ordered that he be turned over to the Franciscan friary of Saint Michael the Archangel at Bordeaux, to be cared for by the monks. Jean was warned that any attempt at escape would result in a trip to the gallows.

*****

SEVEN YEARS LATER

It was 1610. Pierre de Lancre approached the gates of Saint Michael, memories of the Jean Grenier trial running through his mind. He was the one who had sent Jean there, to live the rest of his life in seclusion.

One of the monks met him at the gate and swung it open on squealing hinges. Without a word, the monk turned and walked slowly up the path. De Lancre fell into step beside him, as the monk walked toward a small building near the back of the monastery grounds.

De Lancre asked, "How is he?"

The monk paused for a moment. "He has shown . . . some improvement," he said. "He will now eat our simple food, at times." The monk stopped and placed a hand on de Lancre's shoulder. "When the boy was brought to us, he would only eat the foulest offal from our livestock."

They reached the small building. "We have done the best we can," said the monk. He swung the door open.

Jean, now 20 years old, scrambled back from the light, on all fours. De Lancre stepped into the gloom of the building, which housed a bed and a crude desk. As his eyes became accustomed to the dark, he took in the creature before him.

Jean moved on lean and gaunt limbs; he'd grown taller and skinnier in the time since the trial. He watched de Lancre intently with small, deep-set black eyes.

De Lancre moved closer, and Grenier bared his teeth—some long and white like fangs, others black and broken. He scratched at his head with long, thick, crooked nails.

Jean spoke. "You haven't stopped me. I still change. I still hunt." He gestured toward the monk. "They don't even know when I'm gone." He started to laugh in deep, wracking barks.

De Lancre backed slowly out of the building, his heart heavy. "I've seen enough," he told the monk.

5
THE WEREWOLF OF ANSBACH

Germany, 1685

The people of Ansbach (formerly Anspach) rejoiced. The cruel burgomaster, or mayor, who ran that principality had finally died. They would no longer have to live smothered by his oppressive shadow, enduring the constant fear of retribution for any small infraction, real or invented. Or so they thought.

Although the burgomaster was dead, he had sworn that he never would be gone . . . and something worse took his place shortly after his death.

It began with livestock. Villagers reported missing animals and often found bloody and mangled carcasses in their searches. The bodies, what pieces were found, looked as if they had been torn apart by a large and vicious beast. This went on for some time, and the fear began to return to Ansbach.

Then the first child disappeared. Followed by more children, and more. Women came under attack, and all that was ever found of anyone was savaged remains.

Fear turned to outright terror. Villagers knew what was tormenting them, physically, for they'd seen it in the shadows: a huge, dark wolf, always prowling at the edges of their town.

But spiritually, the timing was too coincidental, too perfect, for the villagers to ignore. Whispers began to circulate. Those whispers became rumor—and then belief. The wolf murdering the people and the livestock of Ansbach was possessed by the late burgomaster, a werewolf in spirit.

The villagers organized a hunt. They brought their dogs and whatever weapons they had at hand, and they fanned out at the edge of the forest. The trees took them in.

Step by step, the villagers-turned-hunters advanced through the undergrowth. The dogs whined and strained, desperate to be unleashed.

Suddenly, the great dark wolf crashed through the villagers' line. The dogs were set loose, and the villagers followed the barks and howls.

They found their dogs circling a well; the wolf had leaped in to escape its pursuers. The beast was finished off, and a loud cheer went up. The villagers knew their time of terror was over.

The wolf's body was taken back to Ansbach, dressed in the burgomaster's clothes, complete with a fake beard and wig, and it was hung from a gibbet. After a time, it was taken down and displayed at a local museum—a reminder to all of what the wolf had really been: the continuation of the burgomaster's terrible rule.

"Werwolf von Neuses" by unknown

6
SAVED BY CHILDHOOD STORIES

Indiana*, USA, 1736

It had been just a few short years since bituminous coal was unearthed along the Wabash River banks. Where there was coal, there was a possibility for work—sometimes a possibility for fortune. Settlers were starting to trickle westward.

Charles Page didn't trust any of them.

He stood on the wooden porch of the trading post, leaning against one of the beams and sharpening his knife. *Now that's something you can trust,* he thought, *a knife.* That and his gun gave him the solid, trusted tools he needed to make a living as a fur trapper.

"Coal," he muttered. He snorted in disgust.

It was silly—all of those grandiose inventions that ran on coal were nothing but stories told to the very young and the very gullible, same as tales of monsters and things that go bump in the night.

Charles inspected his knife, running it against his finger. A single drop of blood welled up, bright red against his weathered skin. He grinned and shoved the knife in its sheath.

He strode into the trading post, approached another trapper, and asked, "Have you heard word of Jean?"

The man shook his head. "No. Last I heard, Jean was still down with fever."

A man of few words, Charles nodded his thanks. His friend, Jean Vatel, had taken sick with a fever three weeks ago and had retreated to his hunting shack in the woods to recover. Charles hadn't seen him since.

He frowned. It wasn't like Jean not to send word. Perhaps Charles would make the trip out to check on him once he was through with his next round of traps.

Several days later, Charles walked through the woods near Vinegar Hill, a lonely path known only to a few. The full moon made the night air shimmer, and it cast sharp shadows across the landscape. Charles stepped lightly, as he always did, his feet making little noise on the forest floor.

He took in a deep breath, enjoying the smells of the earth. In the distance, an undulating cry broke Charles' reverie.

That's strange, he thought. The cry had been similar to a wolf's howl—but not quite right to his experienced ears. He walked on.

Closer this time, the cry echoed through the night.

Charles paused, listening hard as the cry died into silence. *It could be a dog,* he decided, *but it would have to be a big one.*

A shadow darted away from the forest and ran onto the path, blocking Charles' way. A shaft of moonlight caught the creature's black fur, highlighting the tips in silver-gray.

It turned its head toward Charles and stared at him with amber-red eyes.

With some satisfaction, Charles noted that he had been right: It looked like a big dog.

His satisfaction turned to caution. The dog wasn't behaving as most dogs did. It stood, staring at Charles. It wasn't panting, but its lips curled back in a silent snarl.

Not breaking eye contact or showing any weakness, Charles took one soft step to the right.

The dog did the same.

Charles stepped to the left.

The dog echoed his movement.

Time to try a different tack, one that had worked with other predators, including bears. Charles waved his hands above his head and shouted, making himself appear as large as possible. "Out of my way, dog! Begone with you!"

The dog lifted its head back, as if it were laughing, then took three steps toward Charles. It let out another long cry; at this range, the sound was ear-splitting.

Charles didn't flinch. He maintained eye contact as he carefully slung his gun from his shoulder. He didn't want to shoot the animal, but if he had to, he would.

It leaped, closing the distance in an instant. Charles felt the gun torn from his hands as he crashed hard to the ground. The dog's jaws snapped inches from his cheek as Charles fought hard to hold it off. The dog's warm, stinking breath, hot against his face, smelled of sulfur.

"You are no ordinary beast," gasped Charles. His mind raced for an explanation as he struggled to hold the creature back.

He felt his muscles shaking, weakening against the beast's attack. He winced in pain as jaws snapped a hair's breadth from his ear.

Desperate, Charles fixed on a superstitious story from his youth, one about the *loup-garou*, the werewolf. He heard the voice of his grandmother as she told him by a campfire, "A *loup-garou*, Charles, can only be released by blood."

He punched at the beast's throat. It yelped and let up—just enough for Charles to roll to the side and reach for his knife. The beast snarled and launched itself again. As it drove him to the ground, Charles plunged the knife deep into the monster's side. A warm spurt of blood ran down his hand.

"Be released!" he roared.

The beast collapsed onto Charles, howling in pain. Almost at once, the creature grew lighter. Charles shoved it aside and scrambled back, regaining his feet and holding his knife in front of him.

For the first time he could remember, the knife shook in his hand.

The beast writhed on the path, howling and spitting in a shaft of moonlight. Its hair and teeth seemed to melt into its skin, and the snout and ears bubbled and began to shrink. The last to change were the claws, retracting into human-shaped hands.

On the forest floor, panting and moaning, lay Jean Vatel. Blood flowed from a deep wound in his side.

Charles took a step forward. "Jean?" he whispered, not trusting his eyes.

The man nodded.

Relying on practical matters, Charles took off his coat and covered his friend. He quickly bound Jean's wound to stop the bleeding. Then, together, they walked the long path back.

Over the next few weeks, as Jean recovered from his wound, he told Charles he'd been bewitched. It was that, and not a fever, that had sent him into hiding.

Each night for three weeks, he had transformed and roamed the countryside with an insatiable urge to kill and feast. He pleaded with Charles to believe that he'd never harmed people—only livestock and wild animals.

Jean was one of the few people who knew the woods as well as Charles. So Jean had used his last shred of humanity to track Charles to the Vinegar Hill trail.

Like Charles, Jean knew the story of the *loup-garou* from his childhood. It was his last hope that Charles would remember the story and would break the curse through bloodshed. His hope, of course, was met with Charles' trusted knife.

*This account reportedly took place on land that would become part of Indiana, which became a state in 1816.

"Woman & La Bete" by unknown

7
THE BEAST OF GEVAUDAN

France, 1764

Three years of terror—that's what the villagers who lived in the province of Gevaudan endured. From 1764 to 1767, a huge wolf-like creature roamed the woods of the Margeride Mountains, in south-central France, leaving behind a trail of human remains. The wolf was never truly identified, and indeed, some accounts point to the possibility of two wolves working as one.

Whether it was one beast or two, some 210 people were attacked, and 113 of them died by the teeth and claws of a large, savage animal. Many of the victims were found partially eaten.

*****

THE ATTACKS BEGIN

It was June 1, 1764. A young woman walked through an open field, tending to her bulls. A slight rustle from the dark edge of the forest, which bordered the field, gave the woman pause. She cocked her head, listening.

The hairs on the back of her neck rose, and her heart began to pound. Something was coming.

For a moment, she tried to shake off the feeling, silently scolding her own silliness, alarmed only by the wind and waves of leaves.

Then her worst fears burst from the depths of the forest. A huge, reddish-colored wolf, almost as large as her own bulls, streaked straight toward her. It rode on an unspeakable odor, and its enormous claws (attached to human-like hands) tore up the earth as quickly as her eyes could comprehend.

She saw a broad chest, powerful shoulders, spiked ears, and sharp teeth—bared and ready for a meal. The thought of running didn't flit across her mind. She was rooted to the spot, frozen in terror. She didn't even have time to scream before the beast was upon her.

At that moment, for whatever reason, one of her bulls decided to charge. It lowered its sharp horns, and the beast retreated. The woman dashed into the middle of her herd, encircled by the bulls. They would fight to protect themselves and, in doing so, would protect her with their powerful bodies.

The wolf circled the bulls, sniffing, growling, and searching for any sign of weakness. Finding none, it howled and streaked back into the forest.

The young woman had been saved by her herd.

Only 29 days later, the next recorded attack resulted in the beast's first recorded death. Alone, with no other people (and without any animals) there to protect her, a villager named Jeanne Boulet fell victim.

Throughout the coming year, dozens of townspeople were attacked and many children went missing. It was surprisingly common to stumble upon partially eaten remains or to find body parts along the countryside.

More sightings were reported, and it became clear that this was no ordinary wolf.

On one occasion, a shepherd sat atop a small rise, keeping an eye on his flock, making sure they didn't wander too far as they ate their fill of the green grass.

In a blur, a reddish animal was upon them. The shepherd stood and cried out, fearful for his flock and for himself. He waved his arms and shouted, hoping to scare whatever it was away from his precious sheep.

The creature, already huge on all fours, stood and stared at the shepherd. It towered over the bleating, panicked sheep. It reached down and plucked one off the ground as if it were a plaything. The shepherd could only watch, terrified, as the sheep was taken into the dark forest.

At other times and with different encounters, more eyewitnesses said they saw the creature on two legs—running, walking, even wading across a river. Talk began to turn toward a new possibility. The Beast of Gevaudan could be something even more unspeakable than an oversized wolf. The Beast just might be a werewolf.

*****

KING LOUIS XV STEPS IN

By 1765, King Louis XV had heard enough reports of carnage from the Gevaudan province that he charged a trusted soldier, Antoine de Beauterne, with the task of eliminating the Beast.

The soldier traveled to Gevaudan to survey the area, to learn the environment, and to map the Beast's known routes. Then, on September 21, de Beauterne organized a hunting party near the village of Pommier. It consisted of about 40 villagers and a dozen dogs.

De Beauterne held up a hand, signaling for silence. A feeling in his gut said the Beast was near. The wind picked up, rattling the leaves overhead.

There.

Slowly, de Beauterne tracked forward, following the faint odor he'd caught. Another hand signal, and the dogs were released. They surged ahead, barking and howling with the scent of the Beast in their noses.

The men ran after the excited dogs and found them surrounding a ravine. The men spread out and circled it, too, guns at the ready.

The Beast burst from the ravine, and de Beauterne fired, hitting it in the right shoulder. It yelped and spun, searching for a way out. The other hunters opened fire—a deafening sound echoed through the forest. One shot went through the Beast's right eye; it fell still.

A cheer went up, and the men sounded their horn, signaling the end of the hunt. The Beast was dead.

Wasn't it?

As the echoes of the horn died, the Beast rose and charged straight at de Beauterne. With cries of shock and disbelief, again the men fired, and again the Beast fell. This time, it stayed down.

The wolf measured more than six feet and weighed 143 pounds. It's head was enormous, and the fangs were one and a half inches long.

De Beauterne sent a report back to King Louis XV saying, "We declare by the present report signed from our hand, we never saw a big wolf that compared to this one, which is why we estimate this could be the fearsome beast that caused so much damage."

The wolf's body was sent to Versailles, stuffed, and put on display. Villagers from across the Gevaudan province rejoiced and breathed sighs of relief when they heard the good news.

The killings resumed on December 2, 1765, and they came back with a vengeance.

*****

STRANGE REPORTS

Shortly after de Beauterne and the hunting party brought down the wolf, three women of the Gevaudan province walked to church together, as they often did. The path they walked skirted the woods, but it didn't enter the realm of the forest for some way yet. With the sun shining and with the Beast supposedly dead and on display in Versailles, the women felt safe.

As they chatted and walked, a form disengaged from the edge of the forest and materialized in front of them. It was a man, but he seemed to be cloaked in shadows.

The women stopped short, stepping a bit closer to one another.

"May I escort you ladies through the woods?" asked the man. "This is no place to be going alone."

One woman glanced at her friends, then answered for all three. "No, thank you, kind sir. We shall manage as we always have. Good day to you."

The man grinned and said, "As you wish. And good day to you, as well." He touched one of the ladies on the arm and then disappeared back into the forest.

She stood stock still, staring at the place where he'd touched her.

His hand had been covered with fur.

Suddenly, soldiers flew from the forest, just feet from where the man had gone in. The women stumbled back. The soldiers warned the women not to enter the woods; the Beast of Gevaudan had just been spotted nearby, and they were on the hunt.

In another similar story, two women walking to church reported that a stranger had offered to escort them safely through the woods. When they refused, he bowed graciously and bothered them no more. But as the wind tugged at his shirt, they saw that his torso was covered in fur.

*****

AN END TO THE BEAST?

It would be another two long years before an end to the slaughters. A large hunting party was organized on June 19, 1767. Local hunter Jean Chastel joined the party; this region was his home.

Chastel, exhausted from a morning of great effort and little progress, sat by himself in a small clearing.

He settled on a boulder for a few moments, reading and praying. He set his gun at his side, knowing the bullet he'd loaded would serve him well if the time came.

It did, sooner than he could have imagined.

Chastel had just set his Bible aside and had begun to pray when a rustling caught his attention. Huge and reddish-brown, the Beast of Gevaudan crept from the trees and stood, watching Chastel.

Although his heart felt like it would burst from his chest, Chastel finished his prayer and slowly reached for his gun. His eyes watered and his nose dripped from the stench of the Beast.

It watched Chastel's every move yet remained still. Slowly, carefully, Chastel stood. Still the Beast watched. Chastel aimed and squeezed the trigger.

The shot rang through the woods, drawing the other hunters. Chastel had killed the Beast of Gevaudan with one calm shot.

The bullet was pure silver.

Soon after, the Beast was gutted, revealing human remains.

8
THE WOLFMAN ISN'T ALWAYS A MAN

Georgia, 1850s, USA

"Another one?" asked Mrs. Burt. She set her teacup gently on its small plate, paying special attention that her hand didn't shake.

"Several," said Mrs. Evenston. She leaned forward with a conspiratorial air. "Mr. Evenston says they never saw it coming—just found the poor things in the dawn light. Blood everywhere."

For months, sheep had been disappearing from local farmers' flocks, only to be found half eaten, bloodied and mangled, in the morning light. The farmers, assuming it was the work of a rogue wolf, had tried setting traps and also patrolled nightly with their rifles at the ready—so far, to no avail.

"How many does that make?" asked Mrs. Burt.

Mrs. Evenston shrugged. "Plenty. That's all I know." She took a sip of tea. "Oh, hello, Emily."

Mrs. Burt's daughter, Emily Isabella, stood in the doorway of the sitting room. A small child, she was at the awkward age just before her teens, made more so by her bushy eyebrows and decidedly pointed teeth.

"Hello, Mrs. Evenston," she said shyly. "There have been thirteen."

"Thirteen what, dear?" asked Mrs. Evenston.

"Sheep." Emily Isabella fell silent.

"Yes, dear, um, thank you," said Mrs. Evenston. She leaned in again. "I hear, Mrs. Burt, that the men are planning to capture the dreadful wolf responsible once and for all—tonight."

Emily Isabella cried out and fled down the hall. The women heard her footsteps echoing up the staircase.

"What was that about?" asked Mrs. Evenston.

Mrs. Burt smoothed her skirt nervously. "My Emily suffers from dreadful headaches. I dare say it was the onset of one." She stood. "I'm sorry, Mrs. Evenston, but you'll excuse me while I check on her, won't you?"

"Of course, dear, of course," said Mrs. Evenston. "I really must be going, anyway."

Mrs. Burt stood outside Emily Isabella's bedroom, listening to the sobs within. She raised her hand to knock, then let her hand fall. She had a better idea.

Later that night, Mrs. Burt sat in the darkened sitting room. (Her husband had gone out long before as part of the hunting party, set on ridding Talbot County of the wolf's menace.) In her right hand, she clutched her Bible. In her left, a rifle.

She waited.

She listened.

Soon, her wait was over. Mrs. Burt heard soft footsteps come down the stairs and hesitate at the front door. The latch opened, the door squeaked ever so slightly, and the latch fell closed.

Emily Isabella was out again. But where did she go?

Tonight, Mrs. Burt was resolved to find out. She left the Bible on the table and took the rifle with her. She slipped out the door, just moments after her daughter, and caught a flash of Emily Isabella's skirt as she rounded the corner of the street. Through dark alleys and even into the pasture land surrounding the town, Mrs. Burt followed her daughter, just out of sight. At one point, she thought she'd lost Emily Isabella and stopped, panting with the effort of keeping up. Then Mrs. Burt caught sight again of her dark shape running ahead. The chase was still on.

The figure leaped a fence, and a cold stone of fear dropped into Mrs. Burt's stomach. This was Hurley's pasture, full of a healthy flock of sheep.

She clambered over the fence as best she could, still toting her rifle. Was she still following Emily Isabella or some dark creature? Mrs. Burt couldn't tell. All she knew was that her daughter had come this way, and she had to find out where Emily Isabella had gone.

Ahead, sheep bleated in fear. Mrs. Burt hoisted her skirts and ran. As she got closer to the flock, she saw chaos. Sheep scattered in every direction, one following another but none knowing where to go.

A dark shape lunged for one of them. Mrs. Burt, thinking only of Emily Isabella's safety, dropped to one knee, steadied her aim, and fired.

A scream rent the air—not the howl of an animal but the piercing shriek of a girl in pain.

*****

Mrs. Burt watched the whole procedure, watched as the doctor cut off her daughter's hand, so mangled by the shot of a rifle that it had to be amputated.

Two months later, with her stump concealed by a glove, Emily Isabella went to visit family overseas. At least, that's what Mrs. Burt told Mrs. Evenston.

Emily Isabella was gone for quite awhile. Whispers slithered through the social circles, alleging that she was in France, in the care of a doctor who specialized in lycanthropy—in treating werewolves.

The attacks on sheep ceased, and the men of Talbot County celebrated their success in driving off the wolf. However, they had to relinquish that claim in less than a year.

It was about the same time Emily Isabella returned from abroad that sheep once again began to disappear—although not as often as before, as if they were hunted by a wounded predator.

Once in awhile, townsfolk passing by the Burts' house would see a shadowy figure withdraw from the window. Emily Isabella kept to herself there, living in the family home until her death in 1911.

"*Begegnung im Haus* (Werwolf von Neuses)" by unknown

9
GHOST OF THE WEREWOLF

Wales, 1880s

The rowboat's oars slapped into the water, creating ripples that repeated out toward shore. Professor Crewe took in a deep breath of the fresh Merionethshire air; the place was so different from the bustle of Oxford.

This is the life, he thought. No students rallying for good marks on substandard work. No correspondence needing his immediate attention. Just him, his wife Edith, and their friend Arthur Bowen, together at a quaint summer cottage in the beautiful hills of Wales.

Fishing. There was something worthy of immediate attention. A flash of white near the shoreline caught his eye. It was sticking up from the water.

The professor used both oars to pull the boat into a slow glide. "Now that's interesting," he said aloud.

He rowed in for a closer look . . . and couldn't resist. He scooped up the object and shook the sand from it. Staring back at him was a skull. It looked like it had belonged to a large dog, and it was completely intact.

Thrilled with his find, he placed it in the bottom of the boat and rowed on his way, whistling a tuneless melody.

Edith, of course, hated it. "Why in the world would you bring that home, William?" she asked, her hand in front of her nose as if the skull bore some noxious odor.

"It's interesting," her husband replied, placing it on a shelf in the kitchen.

"I agree," said Arthur, breezing into the room, right on cue. "It's part of the colorful local history."

"It's not colorful; it's white," Edith pointed out.

"*Touché, mon chere,*" Arthur said, kissing her hand in mock defeat.

"Oh, get out, both of you," replied Edith. She smiled and shook her head.

William and Arthur bowed as they left. They grabbed their poles and headed in search of fish.

Later that evening, Edith worked in the kitchen, humming and rolling out dough for fresh berry pie.

The hair rose on the back of her neck. She stopped and stood absolutely still.

An odd snuffling sound came from outside the kitchen door. A sudden scratch made her jump. Not normally alarmed at strange happenings, but nervous all the same, Edith ran to the door and threw it open, thinking it must be a neighborhood dog.

Movement at the window caught her attention. She cried out in fright. Although the sunlight was fading fast, Edith saw clearly the head of a huge creature watching her through the glass.

It was half human, half beast, with gaping jaws and sharp, white teeth. Huge paws gripped the window sill like hands. Red, intelligent eyes—human-like eyes—stared at her intently, watching her every move.

Edith stood, frozen in horror, until the creature dropped out of sight and the moment was over. She sprinted for the door and slid the bolt closed. It shook under her hands as something rattled the door latch. She heard heavy breathing, panting, right outside.

Edith backed into the middle of the room. From window to door, to the next window, and back to the door, low snarls circled the cottage while Edith stood terrified, not knowing what to do next.

At last, she heard the sweetest sound of her life: the voices of William and Arthur as they walked through the garden. She wanted to warn them away but found herself speechless.

The kitchen door rattled, and her heart pounded in fright. "Edith, dear," came William's voice, "come and let us in."

She ran to the door and slid the bolt. As William came through, she launched into his arms, clinging to him as if her life depended on it. Arthur edged in, too, looking confused.

"What's this?" said William.

Edith burst into tears. "I know it's silly," she sobbed. "But I know what I saw, and it tried to get in!"

William sat Edith at the kitchen table, brewed her some tea, and had her start from the beginning. As she told her story, both he and Arthur became alarmed.

Later, they sent Edith to bed with strict instructions to rest. Arthur and William sat in the kitchen, mulling over the tale Edith had told. Both men knew better than to suggest Edith had been seeing things; she was the last woman they'd ever accuse of hysterics.

*****

William clutched his gun awkwardly. There wasn't much use for a rifle at Oxford, so he was woefully out of practice. Still, it was some comfort. Arthur held a large stick, the largest he could find in the garden.

Both men were nodding off, their eyes heavy, when a soft sound caught their attention: paws on the gravel outside. William and Arthur looked at one another, fully awake now.

They jumped at the sound of claws screeching down the glass of the kitchen window.

Arthur and William witnessed something from their nightmares. At first, there was a flash of shadowy movement. Then, through the kitchen window, a large wolf glared at them with red eyes. Its gaze raked the kitchen and landed on the skull that William had found earlier that day.

The men rushed to the kitchen door. William flung it open, gun at the ready, but a shadowy shape slipped through the yard's open gate. The two men watched a huge animal race into the lake. It disappeared beneath the surface without causing a single ripple.

At dawn, William rowed back out, onto the lake, the skull resting on the floor of the boat. Arthur and Edith watched from the shore as he hefted the skull and threw it as far into the lake as he could. It hit the water hard and sank.

The wolf never reappeared, until . . .

10
GHOST OF THE WEREWOLF RETURNS

Wales, 1920s

It had been more than 40 years since the professor hurled the strange, dog-like skull into the lake. Jean St. Denis, staying at a small farm in Merionethshire, knew nothing of the terrifying night experienced by the professor's wife, frantically barring the doors against a ghostly, vengeful werewolf.

What she did know was that she was losing light. Jean glanced up from her canvas. The sun's rays were just falling behind the railway station, casting long shadows across the platform where she sketched. She sighed and pushed the hair away from her eyes, leaving a faint black smudge across her forehead. She never got as far as she hoped before the light started to fade.

"There's always tomorrow," she said.

Jean carefully prepared her sketch for the walk home and stowed the foldable easel and her art supplies into her sturdy, green backpack. Since the railway station was deserted, the zipper sounded unnaturally loud in the still evening air.

As she hefted the backpack into place, Jean noticed a truck parked nearby. She squinted in the fading light. Someone was sitting on the back of the truck, looking her way, but she couldn't see the person well. She thought it was a man, but it was as if her eyes kept sliding away when she tried to focus on him.

She remembered with a start—she was alone.

"Do you have the time?" she called out nervously.

The man gave no response.

"Excuse me, sir. Do you have the time?"

Still no response.

Jean walked away as quickly as she could. It was a mile back to the farm, and the shadows lengthened with her every step. She kept her pace quick. Her breathing sped up, got louder. Jean glanced over her shoulder, and she nearly cried out.

Not far back, the strange man followed.

Up ahead, the trees leaned over the road, forming a tunnel as black as tar. It was dark enough now that the man behind her faded to a shadow.

Jean stared into the tunnel and made a decision: no way was she going in there with a strange man tagging along behind her.

She set her backpack on the side of the road and fumbled for her flashlight in its pocket. Then she flipped the switch and whirled around.

Jean screamed. Caught in the beam of her light was a creature unlike any she'd seen before.

Its body was human but strangely shaped—tall and gray. The head was that of a wolf, yellow eyes blazing impossibly bright.

Jean screamed again, scrambling back. Her flashlight jerked upward and caught the creature full in the face. The werewolf's jaws yawned wide as if it were howling in pain. It raised its paw-like hands in front of its face.

There was no sound.

As Jean St. Denis watched, the creature dimmed, faded, and disappeared completely. Quickly, she flung the flashlight beam left, then right, then left again . . .

The werewolf was gone.

"Dore ridinghood"

TALES FROM MODERN TIMES

11
THE WRONG SIDE OF THE TRACKS

Ohio, USA, 1972

Most werewolves attack with claws and teeth, but some choose other, more innovative methods of terror: like two-by-fours.

It had been a very long shift. Ted, a railroad crewman in Defiance, Ohio, worked between two train cars in the early morning hours of July 25. He was looking down, wrestling an air hose into place, when his eyes were drawn to something strange and out of place: two huge, hairy feet, right under the air hose.

The crewman went still, then slowly looked up, following the feet to a pair of blue jeans, a shirt, and a gleaming set of hideous fangs. They were protruding from the snout of an animal's head. The creature also held a two-by-four board slung over its shoulder.

In a blur, the board connected with the crewman's shoulder. He cried out, and the creature ran off. Its scratching, scrambling footsteps created a caveman-like gait as it disappeared into the darkness.

The next day, Ted's coworker Tom laughed at him. "Seriously? A wolfman? You've got to be kidding."

"Just check the roster; see who was working near me," Ted requested.

Tom did as asked, and he quit laughing when all the railroad crewmen were accounted for at the time of Ted's attack. This was no crewmen's joke.

For the next month, several other railroad workers reported similar sightings and attempted attacks, but no one was seriously injured.

*****

In mid-August, a woman woke to the sound of furious scratching at her front door. She sat upright, eyes wide. She glanced at the clock, which read 1:58 a.m.

She had expected the late-night disturbance. Her home near the Defiance railyard had been visited every night for several nights now—always at around 2 a.m.

The doorknob rattled, and something shuffled outside, butting against the front door. Whatever it was, it wanted in.

Just as she did every night, she took a shaky breath and waited for it to be gone.

In the morning light, she decided that enough was enough. She asked her neighbor to call the police and report the incidents. They added it to the large stack of other complaints flooding their office—reports of strange scratching and clawing outside homes, as if something were trying to gain entry.

Drivers of Defiance called in, as well, reporting a creature roaming the roads. They all described it as a tall man with fangs and an animal's head, furry feet, jeans, and a shirt.

It was a few days before reports to the police (and to the local newspapers) began to wane—just as the full moon waned, too.

12
THE DOGMAN IS NO JOKE

Michigan, USA, 1987

"And now, Traverse City, we've got a real treat. A new hit that's sweeping the nation is putting northern Michigan on the map. Take a listen to 'The Legend.'"

Jack O'Malley punched a few buttons and pushed the mic aside. He leaned back in his seat and grinned. It was April 1, 1987. Jack, host of WTCM radio's morning show, along with the show's producer, Steve Cook, had concocted what they thought would be the perfect April Fool's Day prank.

Earlier in the week, Steve himself had recorded "The Legend," a song he and Jack wrote about a half-man, half-dog creature that roamed the wilds of northern Michigan, terrorizing communities.

First one, then another phone light blinked orange. Jack leaned forward as "The Legend" played on. Callers were filling up the lines.

"You're on with Jack O'Malley, WTCM. What's up?"

There was a pause on the other end of the line, a scratchy moment of hesitation. "That song you played, it scared me." The voice carried the crisp, raspy tone of a long-lived life. "It reminded me of something I saw years ago . . ."

And so it began. The elderly man was just the first of many listeners to call in throughout the day and share their own bizarre encounters with the "Dogman."

Although it started as an April Fool's Day joke, "The Legend" quickly became an often requested favorite of WTCM listeners.

Three months later, a forest ranger and a police officer found themselves trekking through the thick northern Michigan woods, responding to a call from the owner of a log cabin outside the town of Luther. They bounced down the twin ruts that passed for a road, branches scraping the sides of the ranger's truck.

"That's got to hurt," said the officer.

The ranger grinned. "It's nothing. This ol' truck has seen a lot worse."

The trees opened up to reveal a log cabin set in a small clearing. A man sitting on the front steps rose at the truck's approach.

"Looks like we're in the right place," said the officer.

The men exited the truck and stepped up to the cabin. The owner shook both their hands.

"Thanks for coming," he said. He led them up the short flight of steps to the front door. "Here's what I wanted you to see."

The ranger let out a low whistle. He reached out a weathered hand and traced the inch-deep furrows in the door frame and surrounding wood.

"It's not just here," said the owner. He led the officer and the ranger on an outdoor tour of the cabin.

Each window had the same markings, which were made by something razor sharp, as if an animal's claws had been working furiously to get in.

"Could a bear make these?" the officer asked.

The ranger considered for a moment, then shook his head in puzzlement. "The spacing's about right. But I've never seen a bear do anything like this—not this deep.

Their claws just aren't sharp enough. It actually even looks like something tried to chew its way in, too."

The officer knelt and touched the ground under one of the windows. "Take a look at this," he told the ranger and the cabin owner.

The men hunkered down to see where he was pointing. In the soft, damp soil under the window was a dog print; it was larger than any dog print the men had ever seen before.

While it wasn't spoken out loud, the thought hit the men at the same time: *Could the tales of the Dogman be true?*

On the way back to town, the officer turned on the radio, perhaps to shake off the sense of unease that had started growing the moment he saw the deep slash marks in the cabin's door frame.

"The Legend" crackled across the airwaves.

"The Werewolf Howls" by Mont Sudbury

13
THE BRAY ROAD BEAST

Wisconsin, USA, 1989

Scott Bray shaded the sun from his eyes with one callused hand. The other rested on his hip as he gazed toward the edge of the field at his dairy farm, outside the town of Elkhorn. The shadow he'd seen a moment before melted away from the trees, giving him a better view.

He sucked in a breath. "Not my herd," he muttered.

He stared at the heavily built animal that lingered in the distance. It looked larger than a German shepherd, with pointed ears and with long, shaggy, gray and black hair covering its entire body. It didn't move quite the way a dog should.

As the peculiar animal wandered near Bray Road on that September day in 1989, it sniffed the air, as if searching for the scent of prey.

Scott Bray had seen enough. "Don't even think about it!" the farmer yelled in challenge to the creature. He would not let his cattle fall victim to the predator.

It glanced in Bray's direction and paused. It seemed to focus and stare straight at him. Then it casually turned and jogged off the other way, along the tree line and out of sight.

A feeling of unease crept into Bray's mind. It was as if he could sense the creature was still there, catching the scent of his dairy herd . . . maybe just biding its time.

Not convinced it would leave his cattle alone (whatever it was), Bray followed its oversized footprints along the edge of his field. He pushed through the trees and onto a rocky outcrop, where the prints ended.

He spun in one direction and the other, searching the ground for a place to pick up the trail. There were no more paw prints to be seen.

Scott Bray had just become the first of many area residents to encounter a monster that would terrorize the region for years to come—a monster that came to be known as the Bray Road Beast.

*****

MIDNIGHT SNACK

Two pools of light swept down Bray Road, ahead of the car. The driver, Lori Endrizzi, navigated the curves as she hummed an almost-familiar melody to keep herself awake.

Suddenly, a dark shape kneeling by the ditch to her right flashed into the beams of her headlights. Lori gasped and tapped her brakes.

"Heck of a place to break down," she said nervously.

Slowing her car, she rounded a curve and coasted closer to the person hunched by the roadside. She hoped he was okay.

Her mind was trying to tell her something—something important—but she was too focused on helping the stranger. She came almost to a stop as she rolled down the passenger side window, intending to call out and ask if help was needed.

Just then, her brain clicked. There was no car nearby, no broken-down vehicle. That's what her mind had been warning her about.

Too late now.

She rolled within six feet of the person. "Hey! Are you—" The rest of her words died in her throat.

At the sound of her voice, a huge, shaggy head swiveled her way. Glowing yellow eyes pinned her in place. That was no person.

The creature bared its fangs, which glimmered at the end of a wolf's snout. With horror, Lori spied the creature's human-like hands; they clutched a mangled lump of bloodied flesh and fur.

She'd seen enough. Lori slammed her foot on the accelerator and sped away, not stopping until she was safely home.

Days later, after the shock of what she'd seen had faded, Lori's curiosity got the better of her. She visited the library to do some research. The pages snicked by as she leafed through books about large predators. She flipped past a page, then turned back.

There it was.

Her fingers trembled as she traced the familiar outline of the creature she'd seen—a creature of legend. It was at that moment Lori knew: She'd crossed paths with a werewolf.

*****

ANOTHER SIGHTING

It was March 1990, just a few short months after Lori Endrizzi's brush with the Bray Road Beast. Dairy farmer Mike Etten blinked and tightened his hands on the wheel of his car. It was well past 2 a.m., and his bed was calling as he sped home along Bray Road.

Just to keep himself awake, he said aloud, "Hospital Road, coming up." But before he got to the intersection, his headlights caught something near the ditch—something large. Suddenly he wasn't so tired anymore. He slowed his car to a crawl for a closer look.

The creature was easily larger than a dog and covered with thick fur. Like Lori before him, Mike saw the beast sitting up and clutching something lifeless in its hands. As the car passed by, the creature tore off a chunk of whatever unfortunate animal was in its grip. Its long snout and thick features tracked Mike's car as it rolled past. Its lips curled back in a snarl.

The image of the creature, illuminated in his headlights, burned into Mike's mind all the way home. He convinced himself it had been a bear, but that didn't quite match what he'd seen. (He was from rural Wisconsin, and he knew about bears.) But what else could it be?

More than a year later, when other people began to come forward at the end of 1991, Etten realized with a jolt that he had probably seen the Bray Road Beast.

*****

THAT'S NO PUPPY

Eleven-year-old Heather Bowey switched her orange plastic sled to the other hand, letting the edge drag through the snow as she and her friends trudged home. She flexed her free hand, getting a little bit of feeling back into her frozen fingers.

Splat!

A cold, wet snowball smacked onto Heather's back. She laughed and, in one smooth motion, leaned down, scooped a handful of slushy snow from the side of the road, whirled around, and hurled it at the culprit behind her. It found its target with a wet and satisfying *smack*.

The group of girls chattered and laughed as they hauled their sleds home. Looking at the sunset, they were just in time: late enough that they'd gotten a good afternoon of sledding and early enough that they wouldn't be in trouble for being out after dark.

It was December 1990, and they were on Loveland Road, not far from Bray Road, where the whispers of something strange were just beginning to surface.

"Hey, check it out," said one of Heather's friends. She pointed toward the stream running parallel to the road, the stubbles of a cornfield poking up through the snow beyond its banks. "Do you know whose dog that is? It's huge."

Heather looked to where her friend pointed. In the distance, a silvery brown animal loped beside the creek.

"I love dogs," exclaimed another friend. "Come over here, puppy!"

Several more girls joined in. "Here, puppy, puppy!"

The animal stopped in its tracks. It cocked its head, first one way, then the other, as if listening to the calls of the girls.

"I think he hears us," said one of the friends.

They continued calling to the animal.

Heather's instincts awakened. For some reason, she didn't want the animal to come any closer. "Hey, guys, I don't think—" Her blood suddenly ran colder than the December air, turning to ice in her veins.

The creature rose to stand on two legs. It looked almost human, staring straight at the group of girls.

Stunned, they fell silent, mesmerized.

The creature took a step forward, then another, and another, each step gaining speed. It dropped to all fours, and it charged.

The spell was broken. Heather screamed, her voice adding to the panicked cries of her friends. As a group, they turned and ran, fast and hard, not daring to look behind them.

They reached Heather's house and piled against the front door. Heather prayed it wasn't locked. Her frozen hands slipped on the doorknob, and she would have screamed again, but she was out of breath.

Finally, her soggy gloves caught, and she felt the door swing open. She and her friends tumbled through and slammed the door behind them.

Heather ran across the living room in her snow-covered boots, leaving a trail of muddy slush in her wake. She peeked out the front window.

No creature in sight.

She breathed a sigh of relief, but not for long.

"Heather Bowey!" Her mother stood in the doorway to the kitchen, hands on her hips and a dangerous look on her face. "What do you think you're doing? Look at the mess you just made."

There was a pause of silence, then all the girls started to talk at once.

After hearing the girls' story, and with all of them reporting the same details, Heather's mother contacted county animal control the next morning.

Heather sat at the breakfast table, listening to one side of the conversation.

"Yes."

"Yes."

"On two legs, that's what they said."

"Yes, all of them."

Five minutes later, her mother hung up.

"What did he say?" asked Heather.

Heather's mother shook her head. "He said it was probably a coyote."

"A coyote!"

Her mother shrugged. "If it wasn't that, I don't know what it was. The main thing is you didn't get hurt."

But Heather knew what she'd seen. It definitely wasn't a coyote. And it was no puppy. Heather and her friends had been chased by a werewolf.

*****

SPOTLIGHT ON THE BRAY ROAD BEAST

The legend of the Bray Road Beast truly sank its claws into the nation with an incident that occurred on (appropriately) Halloween night: October 31, 1991.

About a year and a half after Mike Etten's brush with the beast near Hospital Road, teenager Doris Gipson traveled the same route. However, while Mike tried to convince himself he'd seen a bear, Doris's experience, and the evidence, left no doubt in her mind that she'd come up against a monster.

Bray Road was dark, but Doris's mood was light. It was Halloween, after all. She cranked up the radio as she cruised the familiar road. The music gave way to chatter.

"Ugh—commercials," said Doris. She leaned forward to flip stations, taking her eyes away from the road for only a second.

The wheel jolted under her hands, and the car jerked as her right front tire surged up, then down. Doris cried out, gripping the wheel and stomping on the brakes.

The car skidded to a stop. Doris shifted into park and twisted in her seat, trying to see what she'd hit.

Nothing was there.

She reached for the door handle and pushed her way out of the car. "Please don't let it be a dog, please don't let it be a dog," she repeated. She took a few hesitant steps along the dark and lonely road, peering behind the car and dreading what she'd find.

Still nothing.

"Hello?" she called, immediately feeling silly. The wind rattled through the trees, making her jump. She let out a nervous laugh. Maybe she'd hit a tree branch or something.

A muscular, hairy form appeared from out of the darkness and leaped onto the road. For an instant, Doris stood petrified, the rhythmic *scratch, scratch, scratch* of the creature's claws on the road holding her captive. It moved straight toward her, appearing larger with each and every step.

Doris snapped out of her trance and ran for her car. She yanked the door open and dove inside, then quickly bolted the locks in place. For a moment, all she could hear was her own panicked breath.

Massive claws slammed onto the trunk, and the car lurched. Doris screamed. Fumbling for the ignition, she turned the key, and the car coughed to life. Another slam, another lurch. Panicked, Doris hit the gas, and the engine roared. She shoved the stick into drive, and the car surged forward. There was a high, sharp squeal of claws rending metal. The car jerked as the beast lost its deadly grip.

Doris risked a glance in the rearview mirror. She saw the creature stumble and fall, growing smaller in the mirror as she sped away.

"Honest, this is where it happened," said Doris. She slowed the car to a crawl.

It was later that Halloween night. She'd brought Cassie, a younger family friend, trick-or-treating. Now she was taking the girl home, once again driving down Bray Road.

Doris had already come up with an explanation. "I hit a bear, and when I stopped, it ran right at me!"

"Were you scared?" asked Cassie.

"Well, yeah!"

"Was the bear okay?"

"Okay enough to wreck my trunk! Did you see what it did?"

"No, but—"

Doris cut her young passenger off. "Shh. Wait," she whispered. The car inched forward, and Doris squinted ahead. "Look." She pointed toward a large, dark form on the side of the road. "I think it's still here."

"Let's get out of here. I wanna go home," said Cassie.

Doris shivered, remembering the sound of claws on metal. "No argument from me," she said.

As the car accelerated away from the beast, Cassie peeked out the window. But she didn't speak a word until they pulled into her driveway.

She reached for the door handle, then paused. She turned and looked at her older friend, her eyes large on her pale face. She shook her head. "Doris, I don't think that was a bear."

The next day, Doris shared her terrifying encounters with a neighbor. She showed him the scratches on her car as proof.

Word began to spread among local residents, and soon some of the other witnesses stepped forward with their own bizarre tales, including Lori Endrizzi, Mike Etten, and Heather Bowey.

The reports led a local newspaper writer named Linda Godfrey to pen an article (and eventually a book and a screenplay) about the sightings. Her story was first published on December 29, 1991.

The story spread quickly, growing into a national sensation. The saga of Elkhorn's Bray Road Beast was picked up by larger media outlets.

Tourists began cruising up and down Bray Road in hopes of glimpsing the werewolf. Werewolf-themed souvenirs and werewolf parties became commonplace in the greater Elkhorn area.

Eventually, the sightings and the hype died down, but the story of the Bray Road Beast never fully ended. In the months and years that followed, everyone from magazine writers and tabloid reporters to politicians and Hollywood producers found their way to southeastern Wisconsin. Each hoped to capitalize on the werewolf sensation.

Today, fresh eyewitness accounts are rare, but they haven't stopped. From a young girl trapped in a tree for hours—just out of the beast's reach—to the occasional travelers who spot the monster crossing in front of them, tales of the werewolf continue to surface.

Perhaps these tales are simply the results of overactive imaginations and media hype. Maybe they're the products of attention seekers wishing to become part of this legend. Yet, of course, another possibility exists: Maybe the stories are true.

SELECTED BIBLIOGRAPHY

"10 Real Life Werewolves." *Listverse*. 25 Jan. 2012. Web.

Guiley, Rosemary Ellen. *The Encyclopedia of Vampires, Werewolves, and Other Monsters*. New York: Visionary Living, Inc., 2005. Print.

"Jean Grenier" Werewolf Page. 2010. Web.

Jeffrey, Gary. *Werewolves—Stories of Deadly Shape Shifters*. New York: The Rosen Publishing Group, Inc., 2011. Print.

Maple, Eric; Bown, Derick; Myring, Lynn; Humberstone, Eliott; et al. *The Usbourne Guide to the Supernatural World*. London: Usbourne Publishing, Ltd., 1979. Print.

Ryckert Cook, Colleen. *Werewolves in America*. New York: The Rosen Publishing Group, Inc., 2012. Print.

Stegall, James. "Werewolf Case in Defiance Not Viewed Lightly by Police." *The Blade*. Toledo, Ohio: 2 Aug. 1972. Web.

Summers, Ken. "An American Werewolf in Defiance." *Spooked*. 12 Oct. 2008. Web.

PHOTO CREDITS

Page 4: "Loup-garou" by unknown - "The Werewolf Delusion" by Ian Woodward. Transferred from en.wikipedia; transferred to Commons by User:FunkMonk using CommonsHelper. Original uploader was Dark hyena at en.wikipedia. Later version(s) were uploaded by JasonAQuest at en.wikipedia.. Licensed under Public domain via Wikimedia Commons - http://commons.wikimedia.org/wiki/File:Loup-garou.jpg#mediaviewer/File:Loup-garou.jpg

Page 18: "Werwolf" by Lucas Cranach the Elder - Gotha, Herzogliches Museum (Landesmuseum). Licensed under Public domain via Wikimedia Commons - http://commons.wikimedia.org/wiki/File:Werwolf.png#mediaviewer/File:Werwolf.png

Page 34: "Werwolf von Neuses" by Unknown - Scan aus: Wolfgang Schild – Die Geschichte der Gerichtsbarkeit. Vom Gottesurteil bis zum Beginn der modernen Rechtsprechung, Hamburg: Nikol Verlagsgesellschaft 1997 S. 67 ISBN 3-930656-74-4. Lizenz von: Verlag Georg D. W. Callwey 1980. Licensed under Public domain via Wikimedia Commons - http://commons.wikimedia.org/wiki/File:Werwolf_von_Neuses.png#mediaviewer/File:Werwolf_von_Neuses.png

Page 43: "Woman & La Bete" by Unknown - French Periodical (unnamed). Licensed under Public domain via Wikimedia Commons - http://commons.wikimedia.org/wiki/File:Woman_%26_La_Bete.jpg#mediaviewer/File:Woman_%26_La_Bete.jpg

Page 58: "Begegnung im Haus (Werwolf von Neuses)" by Unknown - Scan aus: Wolfgang Schild – Die Geschichte der Gerichtsbarkeit. Vom Gottesurteil bis zum Beginn der modernen Rechtsprechung, Hamburg: Nikol Verlagsgesellschaft 1997 S. 67 ISBN 3-930656-74-4. Lizenz von: Verlag Georg D. W. Callwey 1980. Licensed under Public domain via Wikimedia Commons - http://commons.wikimedia.org/wiki/File:Begegnung_im_Haus_(Werwolf_von_Neuses).png#mediaviewer/File:Begegnung_im_Haus_(Werwolf_von_Neuses).png

Page 69: "Dore ridinghood". Licensed under Public domain via Wikimedia Commons - http://commons.wikimedia.org/wiki/File:Dore_ridinghood.jpg#mediaviewer/File:Dore_ridinghood.jpg

Page 78: "WeirdTalesv36n2pg038 The Werewolf Howls" by Mont Sudbury - File:Weird Tales volume 36 number 02.djvu. Licensed under Public domain via Wikimedia Commons - http://commons.wikimedia.org/wiki/File:WeirdTalesv36n2pg038_The_Werewolf_Howls.png#mediaviewer/File:WeirdTalesv36n2pg038_The_Werewolf_Howls.png

ABOUT THE AUTHOR

Deb Mercier lives with her family in outstate Minnesota and is the news editor for the *Pope County Tribune*. When not tracking down news stories or taking photos, Deb writes for children and young adults and has seven books to her credit. She loves good pizza, is a certified "bird nerd," and saves turtles from roadways whenever possible.